Everyman;

Oberpfalz

Everyman

Everyman

A MORAL PLAY

NEW YORK

Duffield and Company

1907

University Press · John Wilson
and Son · Cambridge, U. S. A.

¶ Here begynneth a treatyse how the
hye fader of heuen sendeth dethe
to somon euery creature to
come and gyue a counte
of theyr lyues in this
worlde and is in ma-
ner of a morall
playe.

Dramatis Personae

Messenger

God

Death

Everyman

Fellowship

Kindred

Cousin

Goods

Good Deeds

Knowledge

Confession

Beauty

Strength

Discretion

Five-Wits

Angel

Doctor

HERE BEGINNETH A TREATISE HOW THE
HIGH FATHER OF HEAVEN SENDETH
DEATH TO SUMMON EVERY CREATURE
TO COME AND GIVE ACCOUNT OF THEIR
LIVES IN THIS WORLD, AND IS IN MAN-
NER OF A MORAL PLAY

Messenger

I PRAY you all give your audience,
And hear this matter with reverence,
By figure a moral play;
The Summoning of Everyman
called it is,
That of our lives and ending shows,
How transitory we be all day:
This matter is wonders precious,
But the intent of it is more gracious,
And sweet to bear away.
The story saith: man, in the beginning
Look well, and take good heed to the ending,
Be you never so gay:
Ye think sin in the beginning full sweet,
Which in the end causeth thy soul to weep,
When the body lieth in clay.

[1]   [1   ]

Here shall you see how Fellowship and Jollity,
Both Strength, Pleasure, and Beauty
Will fade from thee as flower in May;
For ye shall hear, how our Heaven King
Calleth Everyman to a general reckoning:
Give audience, and hear what he doth say.

God *speaketh*

I perceive here in my Majesty
How that all creatures be to me unkind,
Living without dread in worldly prosperity:
Of ghostly sight the people be so blind,
Drowned in sin, they knew me not for their God;
In worldly riches is all their mind,
They fear not my rightwiseness, the sharp rod;
My law that I showed, when I for them died,
They forget clean, and shedding of my blood red;
I hanged between two, it cannot be denied;
To get them life I suffered to be dead;
I healed their feet, with thorns hurt was my head:
I could do no more than I did truly,
And now I see the people do clean forsake me:
They use the seven deadly sins damnable,
As pride, covetise, wrath, and lechery,
Now in the world be made commendable:
And thus they leave of angels the heavenly company,
Every man liveth so after his own pleasure,
And yet of their life they be nothing sure:
I see the more that I them forbear
The worse they be from year to year;
All that liveth appaireth fast,
Therefore I will in all the haste

Have a reckoning of every man's person;
For, and I leave the people thus alone
In their life and wicked tempests,
Verily they will become much worse than beasts;
For now one would by envy another up eat;
Charity they do all clean forget.
I hoped well that every man
In my glory should make his mansion,
And thereto I had them all elect;
But now I see, like traitors deject,
They thank me not for the pleasure that I to them
    meant,
Nor yet for their being that I them have lent;
I proffered the people great multitude of mercy,
And few there be that asketh it heartly;
They be so cumbered with worldly riches,
That needs on them I must do justice,
On every man living without fear.
Where art thou, Death, thou mighty messenger?

Death

Almighty God, I am here at your will,
Your commandment to fulfil.

God

Go thou to Everyman,
And show him in my name
A pilgrimage he must on him take,
Which he in no wise may escape;
And that he bring with him a sure reckoning
Without delay or any tarrying.

Death

Lord, I will in the world go run over all,
And cruelly out-search both great and small;
Every man will I beset that liveth beastly,
Out of God's laws, and dreadeth not folly:
He that loveth riches I will strike with my dart,
His sight to blind, and fro heaven to depart,
Except that alms be his good friend,
In hell for to dwell, world without end.
Lo, yonder I see Everyman walking:
Full little he thinketh on my coming:
His mind is on fleshly lusts and his treasure;
And great pain it shall cause him to endure
Before the Lord, heaven's King.
Everyman, stand still; whither art thou going
Thus gaily? Hast thou thy Maker forgot?

Everyman

Why askest thou? Wouldest thou wit?

Death

Yea, sir, I will show you; in great haste I am sent
    to thee
Fro God out of his Majesty.

Everyman

What! sent to me?

Death

Yea, certainly:
Though you have forgot him here,

He thinketh on thee in the heavenly sphere;
As, ere we depart, thou shalt know.

Everyman

What desireth God of me?

Death

That shall I show thee;
A reckoning he will needs have
Without any lenger respite.

Everyman

To give a reckoning longer leisure I crave;
This blind matter troubleth my wit.

Death

On thee thou must take a long journey,
Therefore thy book of count with thee thou bring,
For turn again thou cannot by no way:
And look thou be sure of thy reckoning;
For before God thou shalt answer and show
Thy many bad deeds, and good but a few,
How thou hast spent thy life, and in what wise,
Before the chief lord of paradise.
Have ado that we were in that way,
For, wit thou well, thou shalt make none attorney.

Everyman

Full unready I am such reckoning to give:
I know thee not; what messenger art thou?

Death

I am Death, that no man dreadeth;
For every man I 'rrest, and no man spareth,
For it is God's commandment
That all to me should be obedient.

Everyman

O Death, thou comest when I had thee least in mind,
In thy power it lieth me to save;
Yet of my good will I give thee, if thou will be kind;
Yea, a thousand pounds shalt thou have,
And [thou] defer this matter till another day.

Death

Everyman, it may not be by no way;
I set not by gold, silver, nor riches,
Ne by pope, emperor, king, duke, ne princes;
For, and I would receive gifts great,
All the world I might get;
But my custom is clean contrary;
I give thee no respite, come hence, and not tarry.

Everyman

Alas! shall I have no lenger respite?
I may say Death giveth no warning:
To think on thee it maketh my heart sick;
For all unready is my book of reckoning:
But, [for] twelve year and I might have abiding,
My counting-book I would make so clear,
That my reckoning I should not need to fear.
Wherefore, Death, I pray thee for God's mercy,
Spare me, till I be provided of remedy.

Death

Thee availeth not to cry, weep, and pray:
But haste thee lightly, that thou wert gone this
 journey;
And prove thy friends, if thou can;
For, wit thou well, the tide abideth no man,
And in the world each living creature
For Adam's sin must die of nature.

Everyman

Death, if I should this pilgrimage take,
And my reckoning surely make,
Show me, for Saint Charity,
Should I not come again shortly?

Death

No, Everyman, and thou be once there,
Thou mayest never more come here,
Trust me verily.

Everyman

O gracious God, in the high seat celestial,
Have mercy on me in this most need.
Shall I have no company from this vale terrestrial
Of mine acquaince, that way me to lead?

Death

Yea, if any be so hardy,
That would go with thee, and bear thee company:
Hie thee that thou were gone to God's magnificence,

Thy reckoning to give before his presence.
What, weenest thou thy life is given thee,
And thy worldly goods also?

Everyman

I had ween'd so verily.

Death

Nay, nay; it was but lend thee;
For, as soon as thou art gone,
Another awhile shall have it, and then go therefro,
Even as thou hast done.
Everyman, thou art mad, thou hast thy wits five,
And here on earth will not amend thy life;
For suddenly I do come.

Everyman

O wretched caitiff, whither shall I flee?
That I might escape this endless sorrow!
Now, gentle Death, spare me till to-morrow,
That I may amend me
With good advisement.

Death

Nay, thereto I will not consent,
Nor no man will I respite;
But to the heart suddenly I shall smite
Without any advisement.
And now out of thy sight I will me hie;
See thou make thee ready shortly,

For thou mayest say, this is the day
That no man living may 'scape away.

Everyman

Alas! I may well weep with sighs deep:
Now have I no manner of company
To help me in my journey, and me to keep;
And also my writing is full unready.
How shall I do now for to excuse me!
I would to God I had never be got;
To my soul a full great profit it had be;
For now I fear pains huge and great.
The time passeth: Lord, help, that all wrought!
For though I mourn, it availeth nought:
The day passeth, and is almost ago;
I wot not well what for to do.
To whom were I best my complaint to make?
What, and I to Fellowship thereof spake,
And showed him of this sudden chance!
For in him is all mine affiance;
We have in the world so many a day
Be good friends in sport and play,
I see him yonder certainly;
I trust that he will bear me company,
Therefore to him will I speak to ease my sorrow,
Well met, good Fellowship, and good morrow.

Fellowship *speaketh*

Everyman, good morrow, by this day:
Sir, why lookest thou so piteously?
If anything be amiss, I pray thee, me say,
That I may help to remedy.

Everyman

Yea, good Fellowship, yea;
I am in great jeopardy.

Fellowship

My true friend, show to me your mind;
I will not forsake thee, to my life's end,
In the way of good company.

Everyman

That was well spoken and lovingly.

Fellowship

Sir, I must needs know your heaviness;
I have pity to see you in any distress:
If any have you wronged, ye shall revenged be,
Though I on the ground be slain for thee;
Though that I know before that I should die.

Everyman

Verily, Fellowship, gramercy.

Fellowship

Tush! by thy thanks I set not a straw;
Show me your grief, and say no more.

Everyman

If I my heart should to you break,
And then you to turn your mind fro me,
And would not me comfort, when ye hear me speak,
Then should I ten times sorrier be.

Fellowship

Sir, I say as I will do in deed.

Everyman

Then be you a good friend at need;
I have found you true here-before.

Fellowship

And so ye shall evermore;
For in faith, and thou go to hell,
I will not forsake thee by the way.

Everyman

Ye speak like a good friend, I believe you well;
I shall deserve it, and I may.

Fellowship

I speak of no deserving, by this day;
For he that will say and nothing do,
Is not worthy with good company to go:
Therefore show me the grief of your mind,
As to your friend most loving and kind.

Everyman

I shall show you how it is:
Commanded I am to go a journey,
A long way, hard and dangerous;
And give a strait account without delay
Before the High Judge Adonai;
Wherefore, I pray you, bear me company,
As ye have promised in this journey.

Fellowship

That is matter indeed; promise is duty;
But, and I should take such a voyage on me,
I know it well, it should be to my pain:
Also it make[s] me afeard certain.
But let us take counsel here as well as we can,
For your words would fear a strong man.

Everyman

Why, ye said, if I had need,
Ye would me never forsake, quick ne dead,
Though it were to hell truly.

Fellowship

So I said certainly;
But such pleasures be set aside, the sooth to say,
And also if ye took such a journey,
When should we come again?

Everyman

Nay, never again till the day of doom.

Fellowship

In faith, then will not I come there:
Who hath you these tidings brought?

Everyman

Indeed, Death was with me here.

Fellowship

Now, by God that all hath bought,
If Death were the messenger,

For no man that is living to-day
I will not go that loath journey,
Not for the father that begat me.

Everyman

Ye promised otherwise, pardy.

Fellowship

I wot well I said so truly,
And yet if thou wilt eat and drink, and make good
    cheer,
Or haunt to women the lusty company,
I would not forsake you, while the day is clear,
Trust me verily.

Everyman

Yea, thereto ye would be ready;
To go to mirth, solace and play,
Your mind will sooner apply
Than to bear me company in my long journey.

Fellowship

Now, in good faith, I will not that way;
But, and thou will murder, or any man kill,
In that I will help thee with a good will.

Everyman

Oh, that is a simple advice indeed:
Gentle fellows [hip,] help me in my necessity;
We have loved long, and now I need,
And now, gentle Fellowship, remember me.

Fellowship

Whether ye have loved me or no,
By Saint John, I will not with thee go.

Everyman

Yet, I pray thee, take the labour, and do so much
    for me,
To bring me forward, for Saint Charity,
And comfort me, till I come without the town.

Fellowship

Nay, and thou would give me a new gown,
I will not a foot with thee go;
But, and thou had tarried, I would not have left
    thee so:
And as now God speed thee in thy journey!
For from thee I will depart, as fast as I may.

Everyman

Whither away, Fellowship? will you forsake me?

Fellowship

Yea, by my fay; to God I betake thee.

Everyman

Farewell, good Fellowship; for this my heart is sore:
Adieu for ever, I shall see thee no more.

Fellowship

In faith, Everyman, farewell now at the end;
For you I will remember that parting is mourning.

Everyman

Alack! shall we thus depart in deed,
O Lady, help, without any more comfort,
Lo, Fellowship forsaketh me in my most need:
For help in this world whither shall I resort?
Fellowship here before with me would merry make;
And now little sorrow for me doth he take.
It is said, in prosperity men friends may find,
Which in adversity be full unkind.
Now whither for succour shall I flee,
Sith that Fellowship hath forsaken me?
To my kinsmen I will truly,
Praying them to help me in my necessity;
I believe that they will do so;
For kind will creep, where it may not go.
I will go say; for yonder I see them go:
Where be ye now, my friends and kinsmen [lo?]

Kindred

Here be we now at your commandment:
Cousin, I pray thee, show us your intent
In any wise, and do not spare.

Cousin

Yea, Everyman, and to us declare
If ye be disposed to go any whither;
For, wot ye well, we will live and die together.

Kindred

In wealth and woe we will with you hold;
For over his kin a man may be bold.

Everyman

Gramercy, my friends and kinsmen kind,
Now shall I show you the grief of my mind.
I was commanded by a messenger,
That is an high king's chief officer;
He bad me go on pilgrimage to my pain,
But I know well I shall never come again:
Also I must give a reckoning strait;
For I have a great enemy that hath me in wait,
Which intendeth me for to hinder.

Kindred

What account is that which ye must render?
That would I know.

Everyman

Of all my works I must show,
How I have lived, and my days spent;
Also of ill deeds that I have used
In my time, sith life was me lent,
And of all virtues that I have refused:
Therefore, I pray you, go thither with me
To help to make mine account, for Saint Charity.

Cousin

What, to go thither? Is that the matter?
Nay, Everyman, I had liever fast bread and water,
All this five year and more.

Everyman

Alas, that ever I was bore!
For now shall I never be merry,
If that you forsake me.

Kindred

Ah, sir! what, ye be a merry man!
Take good heart to you, and make no moan.
But one thing I warn you, by Saint Anne,
As for me ye shall go alone.

Everyman

My cousin, will you not with me go?

Cousin

No, by our lady, I have the cramp in my toe:
Trust not to me; for, so God me speed,
I will deceive you in your most need.

Kindred

It availeth not us to tice:
Ye shall have my maid with all my heart;
She loveth to go to feasts, there to be nice,
And to dance, and abroad to start:
I will give her leave to help you in that journey,
If that you and she may agree.

Everyman

No, show me the very effect of your mind;
Will you go with me, or abide behind?

Kindred

Abide behind! yea, that will I, and I may;
Therefore farewell till another day.

Everyman

How should I be merry or glad?
For fair promises men to me make;

[2]   [17]

But, when I have most need, they me forsake;
I am deceived, that maketh me sad.

Cousin

Cousin Everyman, farewell now;
For verily I will not go with you:
Also of mine own life an unready reckoning
I have to account, therefore I make tarrying;
Now God keep thee, for now I go.

Everyman

Ah, Jesu, is all come hereto?
Lo, fair words maketh fools fain;
They promise, and nothing will do certain
My kinsmen promised me faithfully,
For to abide with me steadfastly;
And now fast away do they flee:
Even so Fellowship promised me.
What friend were best me of to provide?
I lose my time here longer to abide;
Yet in my mind a thing there is:
All my life I have loved riches;
If that my Good now help me might,
It would make my heart full light:
I will speak to him in this distress:
Where art thou, my Goods and Riches?

Goods

Who calleth me? Everyman? what, hast thou haste?
I lie here in corners trussed and piled so high,
And in chests I am locked so fast,
Also sacked in bags, thou mayest see with thine eye,

I cannot stir; in packs, lo, where I lie!
What would ye have, lightly me say.

Everyman

Come hither, Good, in all the haste thou may;
For of counsel I must desire thee.

Goods

Sir, and ye in the world have sorrow or adversity,
That can I help you to remedy shortly.

Everyman

It is another disease that grieveth me;
In this world it is not, I tell thee so,
I am sent for another way to go,
To give a strait account general
Before the highest Jupiter of all:
And all my life I have had my pleasure in thee,
Therefore I pray thee now go with me;
For, peraventure, thou mayest before God Almighty
My reckoning help to clean and purify,
For it is said ever among,
That money maketh all right that is wrong.

Goods

Nay, nay, Everyman, I sing another song;
I follow no man in such voyages,
For, and I went with thee,
Thou shouldest fare much the worse for me:
For because on me thou diddest set thy mind,
Thy reckoning I have made blotted and blind,

That thine account thou cannot make truly;
And that hast thou for the love of me.

Everyman

That would grieve me full sore,
When I should come to that fearful answer:
Up, and let us go thither together.

Goods

Nay, not so; I am too brittle, I may not endure:
I will follow no man one foot, be ye sure.

Everyman

Alas! I have thee loved, and had great pleasure
All my life-days on my good and treasure.

Goods

That is to thy damnation without lesing,
For my love is contrary to the love everlasting;
But if thou had me loved moderately during,
As to the poor give part for the love of me,
Then shouldest thou not in this dolour have be,
Nor in this great sorrow and care.

Everyman

Lo, now was I deceived, ere I was ware,
And all, I may wete, mis-spending of time.

Goods

What, wenest thou that I am thine?

Everyman

I had, went so.

[20]

Goods

Nay, Everyman, I say no:
As for a while I was lent thee;
A season thou hast had me in prosperity;
My condition is man's soul to kill,
If I save one, a thousand I do spill:
Weenest thou that I will follow thee?
Nay, not fro this world, verily.

Everyman

I had weened otherwise.

Goods

Therefore to thy soul Good is a thief,
For when thou art dead, this is my guise,
Another to deceive in the same wise,
As I have do thee, and all to his soul's reprefe.

Everyman

O false Good, cursed may thou be,
Thou traitor to God, thou hast deceived me,
And caught me in thy snare.

Goods

Marry, thou brought thyself in care,
Whereof I am right glad:
I must needs laugh, I cannot be sad.

Everyman

Ah, Good, thou hast had long my hearty love;
I gave thee that which should be the Lord's above:

But wilt thou not go with me indeed?
I pray thee truth to say.

Goods

No, so God me speed;
Therefore farewell, and have good day

Everyman

Oh, to whom shall I make my moan,
For to go with me in that heavy journey?
First Fellowship he said he would with me gone;
His words were very pleasant and gay,
But afterward he left me alone.
Then spake I to my kinsmen all in despair,
And also they gave me words fair,
They lacked no fair speaking;
But all forsake me in the ending.
Then went I to my Goods that I loved best,
In hope to have found comfort; but there had I least:
For my Goods sharply did me tell,
That he bringeth many in hell.
Then of myself I was ashamed,
And so I am worthy to be blamed:
Thus may I well myself hate.
Of whom shall I now counsel take?
I think that I shall never speed,
Till that I go to my Good Deed;
But, alas! she is so weak,
That she can 'nother go nor speak:
Yet will I venter on her now.
My Good Deeds, where be you?

[22]

Good Deeds

Here I lie cold in the ground;
Thy sins have me so sore bound,
That I cannot stir.

Everyman

O Good Deeds, I stand in great fear;
I must you pray of counsel,
For help now should come right well.

Good Deeds

Everyman, I have understanding,
That thou art summoned account to make
Before Messias of Jerusalem King;
And you do by me, that journey with you will I take.

Everyman

Therefore I come to you my moan to make:
I pray you, that ye will go with me.

Good Deeds

I would full fain, but I cannot stand verily.

Everyman

Why, is there anything on you fall?

Good Deeds

Yea, sir, I may thank you of all;
If ye had perfectly cheered me,
Your book of account full ready now had be.
Look, the books of your works and deeds eke!

Behold how they lie under the feet,
To your soul's heaviness.

Everyman

Our Lord Jesus help me,
For one letter herein can I not see.

Good Deeds

Here is a blind reckoning in time of distress!

Everyman

Good Deeds, I pray you, help me in this need,
Or else I am for ever damned indeed;
Therefore help me to make my reckoning
Before the Redeemer of all thing,
That king is, and was, and ever shall.

Good Deeds

Everyman, I am sorry of your fall,
And fain would I help you, and I were able.

Everyman

Good Deeds, your counsel, I pray you, give me.

Good Deeds

That shall I do verily:
Though that on my feet I may not go,
I have a sister that shall with you also,
Called Knowledge, which shall with you abide,
To help you to make that dreadful reckoning.

[Enter Knowledge.

Knowledge

Everyman, I will go with thee, and be thy guide,
In thy most need to go by thy side.

Everyman

In good condition I am now in every thing,
And am wholly content with this good thing,
Thanked be God my Creature.

Good Deeds

And when he hath brought thee there,
Where thou shalt heal thee of thy smart,
Then go thou with thy reckoning and thy good deeds
    together,
For to make thee joyful at the heart
Before the blessed Trinity.

Everyman

My Good Deeds, I thank thee heartfully:
I am well content certainly
With your words sweet.

Knowledge

Now go we together lovingly
To Confession, that cleansing river.

Everyman

For joy I weep: I would we there were;
But I pray you to instruct me by intellection,
Where dwelleth that holy virtue Confession?

Knowledge

In the house of salvation;
We shall find him in that place,
That shall us comfort by God's grace.
Lo, this is Confession: kneel down, and ask mercy;
For he is in good conceit with God Almighty.

Everyman

O glorious fountain that all uncleanness doth clarify,
Wash from me the spots of vices unclean,
That on me no sin may be seen;
I come with Knowledge for my redemption,
Redempt with heart and full contrition,
For I am commanded a pilgrimage to take,
And great accounts before God to make.
Now I pray you, Shrift, mother of salvation,
Help hither my good deeds for my piteous exclamation.

Confession

I know your sorrow well, Everyman:
Because with Knowledge ye come to me,
I will you comfort as well as I can;
And a precious jewel I will give thee,
Called penance, voider of adversity:
Therewith shall your body chastised be
With abstinence and perseverance in God's service;
Here shall you receive that scourge of me,
Which is penance strong that ye must endure,
Remember thy Saviour was scourged for thee
With sharp scourges, and suffered it patiently:
So must thou, ere thou pass thy pilgrimage.

Knowledge, keep him in this voyage,
And by that time Good Deeds will be with thee;
But in anywise be sure of mercy,
For your time draweth fast; and ye will saved be,
Ask God mercy, and he will grant truly:
When with the scourge of penance man doth him bind,
The oil of forgiveness then shall he find.

Everyman

Thanked be God for his gracious work;
For now I will my penance begin:
This hath rejoiced and lighted my heart,
Though the knots be painful and hard within.

Knowledge

Everyman, look your penance that ye fulfil,
What pain that ever it to you be;
And I shall give you counsel at will,
How your account ye shall make clearly.

Everyman

O eternal God, O heavenly figure,
O way of rightwiseness, O goodly vision,
Which descended down in a virgin pure,
Because he would Everyman redeem,
Which Adam forfeited by his disobedience,
O blessed Godhead, elect and high Divine,
Forgive me my grievous offence;
Here I cry thee mercy in this presence:
O ghostly treasure, O ransomer and redeemer!
Of all the world hope and conduyter,

Mirror of joy, foundation of mercy,
Which enlumineth heaven and earth thereby,
Hear my clamorous complaint, though it late be,
Receive my prayers of thy benignity,
Though I be a sinner most abominable,
Yet let my name be written in Moses' table.
O Mary, pray to the Maker of all thing
Me for to help at my ending,
And save me from the power of my enemy;
For Death assaileth me strongly:
And, Lady, that I may by mean of thy prayer
Of your son's glory to be partiner.
By the mean of his passion I it crave;
I beseek you help me my soul to save.
Knowledge, give me the scourge of penance,
My flesh therewith shall give acquittance;
I will now begin, if God give me grace.

Knowledge

Everyman, God give you time and space!
Thus I bequeath you in the hands of our Saviour;
Now may you make your reckoning sure.

Everyman

In the name of all the Holy Trinity,
My body punished sore shall be,
Take this body for the sin of the flesh;
Also thou delightest to go gay and fresh;
And in the way of damnation thou did me bring,
Therefore suffer now strokes and punishing:
Now of penance I will wade the water clear,
To save me from purgatory, that sharp fire.

Good Deeds

I thank God, now I can walk and go,
And am delivered of my sickness and woe;
Therefore with Everyman I will go, and not spare,
His good works I will help him to declare.

Knowledge

Now, Everyman, be merry and glad;
Your Good Deeds cometh now, ye may not be sad:
Now is your Good Deeds whole and sound,
Going upright upon the ground.

Everyman

My heart is light, and shall be evermore;
Now will I smite faster than I did before.

Good Deeds

Everyman pilgrim, my special friend,
Blessed be thou without end;
For thee is prepared the eternal glory:
Ye have me made whole and sound,
Therefore I will bide by thee in every stound.

Everyman

Welcome, my Good Deeds, now I hear thy voice,
I weep for very sweetness of love.

Knowledge

Be no more sad, but evermore rejoice,
God seeth thy living in His throne above;
Put on this garment to thy behove,

Which with your tears is now all wet,
Lest before God it be unsweet,
When ye to your journey's end come shall.

Everyman
Gentle Knowledge, what do ye it call?

Knowledge
It is the garment of sorrow,
From pain it will you borrow;
Contrition it is,
That getteth forgiveness,
It pleaseth God passing well.

Good Deeds
Everyman, will you wear it for your hele?

Everyman
Now blessed be Jesu, Mary's son;
For now have I on true contrition:
And let us go now without tarrying.
Good Deeds, have we clear our reckoning?

Good Deeds
Yea, indeed, I have here.

Everyman
Then I trust we need not to fear;
Now, friends, let us not depart in twain.

Knowledge
Nay, Everyman, that will we not certain.

Good Deeds
Yet must thou lead with thee
Three persons of great might.

Everyman
Who should they be?

Good Deeds
Discretion and Strength they hyght,
And thy Beauty may not abide behind.

Knowledge
Also ye must call to mind
Your Five Wits as for your councillors.

Good Deeds
You must have them ready at all hours.

Everyman
How shall I get them hither?

Knowledge
You must call them all together,
And they will hear you incontinent.

Everyman
My friends, come hither, and be present,
Discretion, Strength, my Five Wits and Beauty.

Beauty
Here at your will we be all ready;
What will ye that we should do?

Good Deeds

That ye would with Everyman go,
And help him in his pilgrimage:
Advise you, will ye go with him or not in that voyage?

Strength

We will bring him all thither
To help and comfort him, ye may believe me.

Discretion

So will we go with him altogether.

Everyman

Almighty God, loved may Thou be;
I give Thee laud that I have hither brought
Strength, Discretion, Beauty, Five Wits: lack I
    nought:
And my Good Deeds, with Knowledge clear,
All be in my company at my will here;
I desire no more to my business.

Strength

And I Strength will by you stand in distress,
Though thou wouldest in battle fight on the ground.

Five Wits

And though it were thorow the world round,
We will not depart for sweet ne for sour.

Beauty

No more will I unto death's hour,
Whatsoever thereof befall.

Discretion

Everyman, advise you first of all,
Go with a good advisement and deliberation;
We all give you virtuous monition
That all shall be well.

Everyman

My friends, hark what I will you tell;
I pray God reward you in His heavenly sphere:
Now hearken all that be here;
For I will make my testament
Here before you all present:
In alms half my good I will give with my hands twain
In the way of charity with good intent,
And the other half still shall remain:
I it bequeath to be returned there it ought to be.
This I do in despite of the fiend of hell,
To go quit out of his peril
Ever after this day.

Knowledge

Everyman, hearken what I will say;
Go to priesthood, I you advise,
And receive of him in any wise
The holy sacrament and ointment together,
Then shortly see ye turn again hither,
We will all abide you here.

Five Wits

Yea, Everyman, hie you that ye ready were:
There is no emperor, king, duke, ne baron,
That of God hath commission,

As hath the least priest in the world being;
For of the blessed sacraments pure and benign
He beareth the keys, and thereof hath cure
For man's redemption, it is ever sure,
Which God for our soul's medicine
Gave us out of his heart with great pain,
Here in this transitory life for thee and me:
The blessed sacraments seven there be,
Baptism, confirmation, with priesthood good,
And the sacrament of God's precious flesh and blood,
Marriage, the holy extreme unction, and penance;
These seven be good to have in remembrance,
Gracious sacraments of high divinity.

Everyman

Fain would I receive that holy body,
And meekly to my ghostly father I will go.

Five Wits

Everyman, that is the best that ye can do;
God will you to salvation bring,
For good priesthood exceedeth all other thing;
To us holy scripture they do teach,
And converteth man fro sin heaven to reach;
God hath to them more power given
Than to any angel that is in heaven:
With five words he may consecrate
God's body in flesh and blood to take,
And handleth his Maker between his hands,
The priest bindeth and unbindeth all bands
Both in earth and in heaven;

He ministers all the sacraments seven:
Though we kiss thy feet, thou wert worthy:
Thou art the surgeon that cureth sin deadly,
No remedy may we find under God,
But all only priesthood.
Everyman, God gave priest[s] that dignity,
And setteth them in His stead among us to be;
Thus be they above angels in degree.

Knowledge

If priests be good, it is so surely,
But when Jesu heng on the cross with great smart,
There he gave us out of his blessed heart
The same sacrament in great torment.
He sold them not to us, that Lord omnipotent;
Therefore Saint Peter the Apostle doth say,
That Jesus' curse hath all they,
Which God their Saviour do buy or sell,
Or they for any money do take or tell,
Sinful priests giveth the sinners example bad,
Their children sitteth by other men's fires, I have
    heard,
And some haunteth women's company,
With unclean life, as lusts of lechery;
These be with sin made blind.

Five Wits

I trust to God, no such may we find:
Therefore let us priesthood honour,
And follow their doctrine for our soul's succour;
We be their sheep, and they [our] shepherds be,
By whom we all be kept in surety.

[35]

Peace! for yonder I see Everyman come,
Which hath made true satisfaction.

Good Deeds

Methink it is he indeed.

Everyman

Now Jesu Christ be your alder speed!
I have received the sacrament for my redemption,
And then mine extreme unction;
Blessed be all they that counselled me to take it:
And now, friends, let us go without longer respite;
I thank God that ye have tarried so long.
Now set each of you on this rod your hand,
And shortly follow me;
I go before, there I would be:
God be our guide.

Strength

Everyman, we will not fro you go,
Till ye have gone this voyage long.

Discretion

I Discretion will bide by you also.

Knowledge

And though this pilgrimage be never so strong,
I will never part you fro:
Everyman, I will be as sure by thee,
As ever I was by Judas Maccabee.

Everyman

Alas! I am so faint I may not stand,
My limbs under me do fold:
Friends, let us not turn again to this land,
Not for all the world's gold;
For into this cave must I creep,
And turn to the earth, and there to sleep.

Beauty

What, into this grave? Alas!

Everyman

Yea, there shall ye consume more and less.

Beauty

And what, should I smother here?

Everyman

Yea, by my faith, and never more appear;
In this world live no more we shall,
But in heaven before the highest Lord of all.

Beauty

I cross out all this: adieu, by Saint John;
I take my cap in my lap, and am gone.

Everyman

What, Beauty? whither will ye?

Beauty

Peace! I am deaf, I look not behind me,
Not, and thou wouldst give me all the gold in thy
chest.

Everyman

Alas! whereto may I now trust?
Beauty doth fast away hie:
She promised with me to live and die.

Strength

Everyman, I will thee also forsake and deny,
The game liketh me not at all.

Everyman

Why then ye will forsake me all:
Strength, tarry, I pray you, a little space.

Strength

Nay, sir, by the rood of grace,
I will hie me from thee fast,
Though thou weep till thy heart brast.

Everyman

Ye would ever bide by me, ye said.

Strength

Yea, I have you far enough conveyed:
Ye be old enough, I understand,
Your pilgrimage to take on hand;
I repent me, that I hither came.

Everyman

Strength, you to displease I am to blame;
Yet promise is debt; this ye well wot.

Strength

In faith, as for that I care not:
Thou art but a fool to complain;
Thou spendest thy speech and wasteth thy brain:
Go, thrist thee into the ground.

Everyman

I had ween'd surer I should you have found:
But I see well, he that trusteth in his Strength,
Is greatly deceived at the length;
Both Strength and Beauty hath forsaken me,
Yet they promised me steadfast to be.

Discretion

Everyman, I will after Strength be gone;
As for me, I will leave you alone.

Everyman

Why, Discretion, will ye forsake me?

Discretion

Yea, in faith, I will go fro thee;
For when Strength is gone before,
Then I follow after evermore.

Everyman

Yet, I pray thee, for love of the Trinity,
Look in my grave once piteously.

Discretion

Nay, so nigh will I not come.
Now farewell, fellows everichone.

Everyman

Oh, all thing faileth, save God alone,
Beauty, Strength, and Discretion;
For, when Death bloweth his blast,
They all run fro me full fast.

Five Wits

Everyman, of thee now my leave I take;
I will follow the other, for here I thee forsake.

Everyman

Alas! then may I both wail and weep;
For I took you for my best friend.

Five Wits

I will no lenger thee keep:
Now farewell, and here an end.

Everyman

Now, Jesu, help! all hath forsaken me.

Good Deeds

Nay, Everyman, I will abide with thee,
I will not forsake thee indeed;
Thou shalt find me a good friend at need.

Everyman

Gramercy, Good Deeds, now may I true friends see
They have forsaken me everychone;
I loved them better than my good deeds alone:
Knowledge, will ye forsake me also?

Knowledge

Yea, Everyman, when ye to death shall go;
But not yet for no manner of danger.

Everyman

Gramercy, Knowledge, with all my heart.

Knowledge

Nay, yet I will not from hence depart,
Till I see where ye shall be come.

Everyman

Methinketh, alas! that I must be gone
To make my reckoning, and my debts pay;
For I see my time is nigh spent away.
Take ensample, all ye that this do hear or see,
How they that I loved best now forsake me;
Except my Good Deeds, that bideth truly.

Good Deeds

All earthly things is but vanity,
Beauty, Strength, and Discretion do man forsake,
Foolish friends and kinsmen, that fair spake;
All fleeth save Good Deeds, and that am I.

Everyman

Have mercy on me, God most mighty,
And stand by me, thou mother and maid Mary.

Good Deeds

Fear not, I will speak for thee.

Good Deeds

Short our end and minish our pain:.
Let us go, and never come again.

Everyman

Into thy hands, Lord, my soul I commend,
Receive it, Lord, that it be not lost;
As thou me boughtest, so me defend,
And save me fro the fiend's boast,
That I may appear with that blessed host
That shall be saved at the day of doom:
In manus tuas, of might most,
For ever commendo spiritum meum.

[*Everyman dies.*

Knowledge

Now hath he suffered that we all shall endure:
The Good Deeds shall make all sure;
Now hath he made ending,
Methinketh that I hear angels sing,
And make great joy and melody,
Where Everyman's soul shall received be.

The Angel

Come, excellent elect spouse to Jesu,
Here above thou shalt go,
Because of thy singular virtue:
Now thy soul is taken thy body fro,
Thy reckoning is crystal clear;

Now shalt thou into the heavenly sphere,
Unto the which all ye shall come
That liveth well, after the day of doom.

Doctor

This memory all men may have in mind;
Ye hearers, take it of worth, old and young,
And forsake pride, for he deceiveth you in the end,
And remember Beauty, Five Wits, Strength, and
    Discretion,
They all at last do Everyman forsake,
Save his Good Deeds; [them he] there doth take:
But beware, for, and they be small,
Before God he hath no help at all;
None excuse may be there for Everyman:
Alas, how shall he do then?
For after death amends may no man make,
For then mercy and pity doth him forsake;
If his reckoning be not clear, when he doth come,
God will say, Ite, maledicti, in ignem æternum;
And he that hath his account whole and sound,
High in heaven he shall be crowned;
Unto which place God bring us all thither,
That we may live body and soul together;
Thereto help the Trinity:
Amen, say ye, for Saint Charity.

315

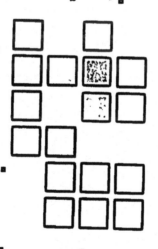

Lightning Source UK Ltd.
Milton Keynes UK
UKOW05f1814010617
302500UK00015B/276/P